Nelson

SPELLING

D0316058

PUPIL BOOK 2

JOHN JACKMAN

Nelson

Book 2 – Contents/Scope and Sequence

Page	Focus	Extra	Extension	Focus pcm	Extension pcm
					*specials
4/5￼Unit 1	Flashback!￼blend + magic e￼ow/ou/oa/oy/ar/￼ss/wa	e + ing￼sh/ch	there/their￼vowel letters￼silent k￼y + ed		
6/7￼Unit 2	old	old + er	alphabet – letter￼order	initial letter + old￼word building	alphabet – letter￼order
8/9￼Unit 3	wh	words within wh￼words	compound words	initial wh word￼building	*what/who/whose￼cloze￼hidden wh words
10/11￼Unit 4	ear￼ead	simple definitions￼puzzle	longer ea words￼wordsearch	initial letter/blend￼+ ear/ead word￼building	sorting ea sound￼families￼ea homophones￼cloze
12/13￼Unit 5	nch￼tch	tch + ing verbs	ch + es rule	matching￼copying￼rhyme	tch/nch in medial￼position￼ch, sh, s, x plurals￼(+ es)
14/15￼Unit 6	er	ever/every words	+ er rules	final er word￼building	+ er/ed/ing consonant￼doubling rule
16/17￼Unit 7	oi￼oy	oil/oin/oy letter￼pattern families	oi/oy puzzle	oil/oin/oint/oy￼patterns￼matching, rhyme	using oi/oy words
18/19￼Unit 8	oo	oom/ook/ood/oor￼patterns	alphabetical order￼(initial letter)	ook/oot/ood/oor/ool￼patterns￼matching, rhyme	alphabetical order￼(initial letter)
20/21	*Check-up 1*	*Check-up 1*	*Check-up 1*	*Check-up 1*	*Check-up 1*
22/23￼Unit 9	ou(nd)	your, you're￼contractions	alphabetical order	initial letter + ound￼word building￼matching	*could/would/should￼cloze￼ou type homophones
24/25￼Unit 10	ar￼are	ar/are letter￼pattern families	er/fully/ful/ly/ing/d￼suffixes	initial letter/blend￼+ art/are word￼building	suffixes

Page	Focus	Extra	Extension	Focus pcm	Extension pcm
					*specials
26/27 Unit 11	or ore	ed/d rule	oor/aw/ore/our sounds puzzle	ork/orn/ort/ore patterns matching, rhyme	or word puzzles
28/29 Unit 12	aw	simple definitions puzzle	aw/oar/ore/our/oor sounds puzzle	initial letter/blend + aw word building	similar sounds cloze
30/31 Unit 13	ew	ew hidden words (puzzle)	alphabetical order (second letter)	initial letter/blend + ew word building	alphabetical order (second letter)
32/33 Unit 14	silent letters – final b/initial k	final b + ing/ed	suffix + final letter doubling rule	final mb, initial kn word building	silent letters
34/35 Unit 15	y endings (nouns)	simple definitions puzzle	y ending plurals (ies)	final y patterns word building	y ending + plurals making adjectives
36/37	Check-up 2	Check-up 2	Check-up 2	Check-up 2	Check-up 2
38/39 Unit 16	ir ire	ir/ire letter pattern families	dictionary definitions	ird/irt/irst/ire patterns matching, rhyme	guide words alphabetical order
40/41 Unit 17	ur ure	ur words cloze passage	ur pattern wordsearch + ing	medial ur word building	ur/ir/er pattern puzzles
42/43 Unit 18	ai ay	compound words	homophones	ai/ay patterns matching, rhyme	*said/says/again cloze hidden ai/ay words puzzle
44/45 Unit 19	ain air	air homophones cloze exercise	air compound words	initial letter/blend + ain/air word building	air/are cloze and definitions
46/47 Unit 20	igh	simple definitions puzzle	+ er/est suffixes igh/y words	initial letter/blend + ight word building	making adverbs (+ly) homophones
48	Check-up 3	Check-up 3	Check-up 3	Check-up 3	Check-up 3

Flashback!

Focus FLASHBACK

Find the missing letters.
Write the words in your book.

1 b _____

2 r _____

3 s _____

4 c _____

5 ch _____

6 s _____

7 c _____

8 m _____

9 g _____

10 b _____

11 d _____

12 s _____

13 w _____

14 s _____

15 g _____

16 m _____

Extra

Do you remember what happens to magic e words before adding **ing**?

A Add *ing* to these words.

ride   wave   make
drive   face   trace

B Make words with these letters by adding *ch* or *sh*.

__ick   __ell   __ut   mu__   fi__

Extension

A Write a sentence for each group of words.

1 here   there
2 his   hers   their

B Copy this sentence and put in the missing vowel letters.

"I hav__ mad__ panc__k__s f__r t___," sa__d D__d.

C A silent letter is missing from these words. Write them correctly.

__nock   __nife   __nob

D Add **ed** to these words.
Remember, you need to change one of the letters.

cry   fry   try   spy

5

old

old

SPELLING *Focus*

key words

look say cover write check

old
cold
fold
gold
hold
sold
told
scold

check write cover say look

A Look at these picture clues.
Write the **old** words in your book.

1 g_____

2 f_____

3 h_____

4 c_____

B Copy four more **old** key words neatly into your book.

C Write a sentence that uses at least two of the key words.

6

old   cold   fold   hold

1 Add *er* to the end of each word in the box. Write the words you have made in your book.

2 Write a sentence for each word.

3 Put as many of the words as possible into a funny, nonsense sentence.

SPELLING *Extension*

Here is **the alphabet**.

a b c d e f g h i j k l m n o p q r s t u v w x y z

Copy these letters and fill in the gaps.

1 a _ c d   2 e f _ _

3 s _ u _   4 _ n o _

Use the alphabet to help you.

Sort these letters so that they come in the order they would in the alphabet. The first one is done to help you.

1 c a d b   a b c d   2 e g f h

3 u s t r   4 j i l k

5 z y x w   6 r p q o

7 l j g e   8 y w t z

7

wh

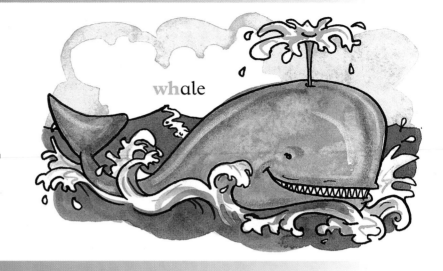

whale

key words

look say cover write check

check write cover say look

when

where

wheel

wheat

which

whip

while

white

why

Copy these questions.
Choose **wh** key words to fill the gaps.
Start each sentence with a capital letter.

1 _____ are we going?

2 _____ will the bus come?

3 _____ bus are we catching?

4 _____ isn't Dean coming with us?

8

A How many small words can you find in these **wh** words? For example: **where** gives **he** (w**he**re); **her** (w**her**e); **here** (w**here**).

Now try these. The picture clues may help you.

1 *wheel*   2 *white*   3 *wheat*   4 *when*

B Write four questions that you would like to ask your teacher.
Begin each question with a **wh** word.

Make as many **compound words** as you can using these words. The first is done to help you.
Beware, one doesn't work!

It's usual **not** to make a compound word of **no one**.

no		
every	where	nowhere
any	+ one	
some	thing	

Write three sentences using one word from each group you have made.

9

ear
ead

head

ear

SPELLING *Focus*

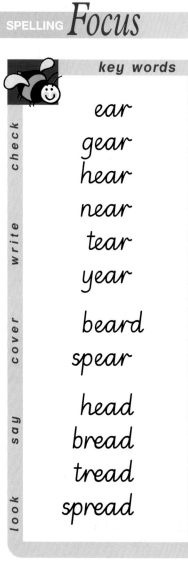

key words

look say cover write check

ear
gear
hear
near
tear
year

beard
spear

head
bread
tread
spread

A Look at these picture clues.
Write the **ear** or **ead** words in your book.

1 t _____   2 _____

3 h _____   4 br _____

B Write four other **ear** key words neatly into your book.

C Write a sentence that uses at least two of the key words.

10

The answer to each clue is an **ear** or **ead** key word.
Write them in your book.

1 I have a sharp point.
2 I have 12 months.
3 I'm good to eat if I'm fresh.
4 I am part of your body.
5 I have a twin on the other side of your head.
6 I'm the opposite of **far**.

SPELLING *Extension*

A Find the 11 words hidden in this puzzle where
ea sounds like 'e' in bed.
Copy them into your book.

f	e	a	t	h	e	r	t
l	z	p	w	e	x	e	u
e	b	r	e	a	d	a	s
a	d	e	a	v	e	d	t
t	e	a	t	y	a	w	e
h	a	d	h	l	d	s	a
e	f	y	e	m	r	v	d
r	a	l	r	e	a	d	y

B One word in the puzzle can be said in two
different ways. Which word is it?

11

nch
tch

pinch

witch

SPELLING *Focus*

key words

look say cover write check

catch
hatch
match

itch
pitch
witch

hutch

finch
pinch

bunch
hunch
punch

check write cover say look

A Find words that rhyme with these. The picture clues will help. Write the answers in your book.

hatch

ditch

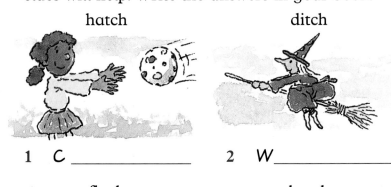

1 c _____

2 w _____

finch

lunch

3 p _____

4 p _____

B Write three other **tch** and three other **nch** words neatly in your book.

C Write a sentence that has one **tch** and one **nch** word in it.

Look at the words in the box.

> snatching scratching sketching
> stretching stitching switching

Find a word in the box to match each picture.

1

2

3

4

5

6

Write sentences about three of the pictures.

SPELLING *Extension*

Plural means more than one.

If a noun ends in **ch** we add **es** to make it plural, like this:

one match   three match**es**

A Make these words plural.

scratch sketch ditch pitch witch stitch switch
finch bunch lunch punch bench patch hutch

B Say the words to yourself.
Can you think why we add **es** and not just **s** to make **ch** words plural?

er

summer

swimmer

key words

look say cover write check

look say cover write check

her
herd
kerb

ever

every

under
teacher
flower
singer

hammer
letter
swimmer

A Look at the pictures.
Write the rhyming key words in your book.
The first one is done to help you.

1 **power** rhymes with  *flower*

2 **better** rhymes with

3 **slimmer** rhymes with

4 **preacher** rhymes with

B Write five other **er** key words neatly in your book.

C Write a sentence that has at least two of the key words in it.

A Use *ever* to make new words.

n _____   _____y

Don't forget your
capital letters and
full stops!

B Use *every* to make new compound words.

_____one _____where _____thing

C Write three sentences using some of the words
you have made.

Sometimes we must double the last letter of a
word before we add **er**.

   run   runner   dig   digger

Look at the letter before the last letter.
Is it a single vowel (**a e i o u**)?

r<u>u</u>n	yes	r<u>u</u>**n**ner
sh<u>o</u>p	yes	sh<u>o</u>**pp**er
si<u>n</u>g	no	si**n**ger
r<u>ea</u>d	no, there are two	r<u>ea</u>**d**er

Add *er* to these words.
The underlines will help you.

1 s<u>i</u>t   2 w<u>i</u>n   3 fl<u>i</u>p   4 sw<u>i</u>m

5 sp<u>i</u>n   6 tr<u>a</u>p   7 ta<u>n</u>k   8 st<u>o</u>p

9 sma<u>c</u>k   10 sp<u>ea</u>k   11 ba<u>n</u>g   12 wa<u>l</u>k

15

oi
oy

coin

boy

SPELLING *Focus*

key words

look say cover write check

check write cover say look

oil
boil
soil

coin
join
joint
point
choice
voice

boy
joy
toy

A Look at the pictures.
Write the rhyming key words in your book.
The first one is done to help you.

1 **join** rhymes with   *coin*

2 **joy** rhymes with

3 **joint** rhymes with

4 **soil** rhymes with

B Write five other **oi** key words neatly in
your book.

C Write a sentence that has at least two of the
key words in it.

16

> join boil joint oiled joy joined
> spoiling soil coin toy spoil
> point boys oil oily pointing
> enjoy spoilt

A Sort the words in the box into letter pattern families, like this:

oil words	oin words	oy words
soil	joint	toy

B Write three sentences using at least one word from each letter pattern family.

SPELLING *Extension*

Copy these words, filling the gaps with **oi** or **oy**.

1 s____l   earth

2 c____ns   money

3 p____nt   a sharp end

4 j____n   fix together

5 v____ce   used for speaking and singing

6 enj____   to take pleasure

7 t____s   children play with these

oo

The cook
Reading book
About spooks
Looks
Frightened.

Constance Milburn

SPELLING *Focus*

key words

look say cover write check

book
cook
look
took
crook
shook
foot
soot
good
wood
door
floor

A Look at these picture clues.
Write the **oo** words in your book.

1 h_____

2 b_____

3 w_____

4 h_____

B Write four other **oo** key words neatly in your book.

C Look at the poem.
Make a list of words that have the **oo** pattern.

How many words can you make by mixing these patterns with the letters?

For example, **r + oom = room**;
br + oom = broom

Letters box	**Pattern box**
b br r p d h fl	oom ook
c cr l t sh w	ood oor

Look in your dictionary to check any words you're not sure about.

When we put words in **alphabetical order**, we start by putting them in the order of their first letters, like this:

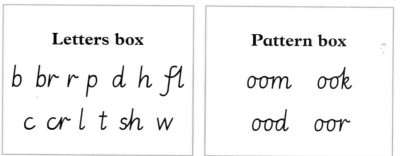

| boom | doom | room | zoom |

Write these words in alphabetical order.

1 look cook took

2 wood hood good

3 poor door floor

4 crook shook brook

Check-up 1

Write a word from the box that rhymes with each of these words.
The pictures will help you. The first one is done for you.

old

bread

hear

1 <u>cold</u>   2 _____   3 _____

patch

ditch

lunch

4 _____   5 _____   6 _____

power

better

floor

7 _____   8 _____   9 _____

letter
match
ear
cold
pitch
door
flower
head
punch

20

Remember the question mark to finish each sentence.

A Use each of these question words at the beginning of a sentence.

1 When 2 Where 3 Why 4 Which

B Write all the compound words you can think of that have **every** in them.
Here is one to get you started – *everybody*

C Write the smaller words you can find in each of these words.

1 enjoyable 2 pointing 3 unspoiled

A Sort these letters so that they come in the order they would in the alphabet. The first one is done to help you.

1 c a d b = a b c d 2 e g f h

3 z y o v p t 4 s r m i p k

Remember, **plural** means more than one.

B Make these words plural.

1 dog 2 boy 3 girl
4 punch 5 bench 6 ditch
7 finch 8 patch 9 hutch
10 scratch

C Add *er* to these words. Remember, you may need to double the last letter in some of the words.

1 win 2 swim 3 walk 4 flip 5 bang

ou

thought

hound

SPELLING *Focus*

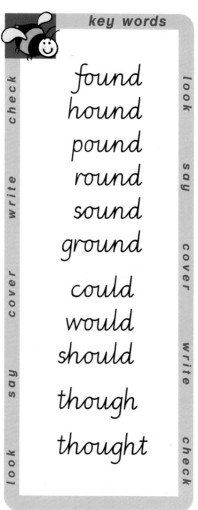

key words

look · say · cover · write · check

found
hound
pound
round
sound
ground

could
would
should

though

thought

look · say · cover · write · check

A Look at these pictures. The words that go with them all rhyme with **pound**.
Write the words in your book.

1 f _____

2 r _____

3 g _____

4 s _____

B Make a list of the key words where the **ou** letter pattern makes a different sound.

C Write a sentence that has at least two **ou** words in it.

Contraction
means a shorter
word.

Sometimes we run words together as we speak. This makes new words, called **contractions**. If we say **you** and **are** together it's written **you're**. The ' shows where something has been left out.

A Read these sentences quietly to yourself. Try putting in **you are** or **your**. Which one makes sense?
Copy the sentences into your book, choosing *you're* (which means **you are**) or *your* to finish them.

1 Can I come to _____ party?

2 No, _____ too young.

3 I think _____ being unkind.

4 _____ wrong!

5 But _____ Dad said I am old enough.

Remember, when we make **contractions** we make one word from two, e.g. **did not = didn't**.

B Make contractions from these pairs of words.

1 should not   2 could not

3 would not

Use each contraction in a sentence.

SPELLING *Extension*

Look at the words in the box.
Write them in **alphabetical order**.

found   hound   sound   round   ground   pound

ar
are

car

rare

SPELLING *Focus*

key words

look say cover write check

look say cover write check

car
cart
bar
bark
barn

art
smart
start

care
rare
scare
share

A Look at these picture clues.
Write the **ar** or **are** words in your book.

1 c_____

2 c_____

3 sh_____

4 sc_____

B Look at the key words. Copy four with the **art** letter pattern neatly into your book.

C Write a sentence that uses at least two of the key words.

Sort the key words into sound pattern families, like this, and write them in your book:

words with **ar** sounding like c**ar**	words with **are** sounding like c**are**
barn	fare

Write a sentence using one word from each family.

SPELLING *Extension*

A Put one ending on each word, without changing any spellings, like this:

care + fully = carefully

You need to think very **carefully**!

word box	**endings box**
care art start scare smart bark	er fully ful ly ing d

B Write sentences using three of the words you have made.

25

or ore

SPELLING *Focus*

key words

look say cover write check

cork
fork
born
horn
torn
fort
short
sport
horse
more
sore
wore

look say cover write check

A Find words that rhyme with these. The picture clues will help. Write the answers in your book.

gorse

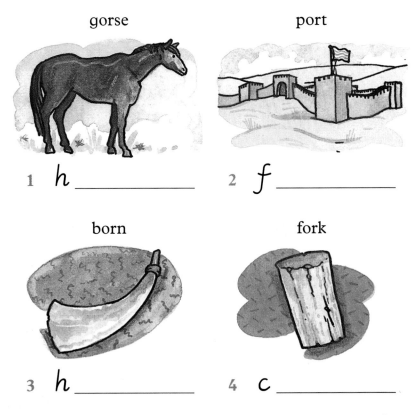

port

1 h_____

2 f_____

born

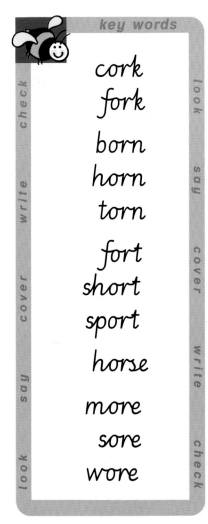

fork

3 h_____

4 c_____

B Make a list of at least four other **or** or **ore** words that you can find in the picture at the top.

We add **ed** to a verb when something has already happened, like this:

"Will you sort your toys out?" said his mother.
"I sort**ed** them out yesterday," he said.

If the verb already ends in **e** then just add **d**, like this:

snor**e**   snor**ed**

A Add *ed* or *d* to these words.

store   cork   force   scorch   score

B Write these sentences, changing them so that the action has already happened.

1 I will force the door open.

2 The hot iron will scorch the shirt.

3 I will score two goals!

These three words have similar sounds.
poor   **paw**   **pour**
They have **different** spellings.

for four more moor wore war or ore horse hoarse

A Write a word from the box to match each clue.
1 an animal with four legs
2 one more than two less than five
3 when armies fight
4 a type of rock
5 opposite of less

B Can you think of other words that have similar sounds but different spellings? Write them in your book.

27

aw

paw

draw

SPELLING *Focus*

key words

look say cover write check

law
paw
saw
claw
draw
thaw
lawn
yawn
spawn
crawl
trawl
shawl

A What are they doing? Look at these picture clues. Write the **aw** words in your book.

1 s _____ ing

2 dr _____ ing

3 y _____ ing

4 cr _____ ing

B Write four other **aw** key words neatly in your book.

C Write a sentence that uses one of the **ing** words you have written.

28

A Solve these puzzles.
Clue: each answer is a key word!

1 It has sharp teeth, but not for eating.
2 A cat has four of these.
3 We do this when we feel tired.
4 Babies do this before they learn to walk.
5 You can do this with a pencil.

B Now make up three more puzzles about **aw**
words for a friend to solve.

SPELLING *Extension*

These two words have similar sounds.
   raw   **roar**
They have **different** meanings and spellings.

saw sore   law lore

paw poor pour flaw floor

Choose a word from the box to match each clue.

1 a cat's foot
2 tip liquid from a container
3 a grazed knee will feel like this
4 has little money
5 something you mustn't break
6 we walk all over it

ew

I kn**ew**
A **ewe**
  Who ate st**ew**
  As she fl**ew**
  In a n**ew**
  Hovercraft.
    Some people
    Are daft.

Constance Milburn

SPELLING *Focus*

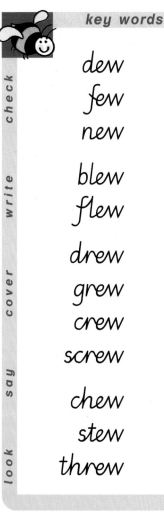

key words

look   say   cover   write   check

dew
few
new
blew
flew
drew
grew
crew
screw
chew
stew
threw

look   say   cover   write   check

A Look at these picture clues.
Write the **ew** words in your book.

1 n _____

2 d _____

3 s _____

4 ch _____

B Write six other **ew** key words neatly in your book.

C Look at the poem.
Make a list of the **ew** words.

30

Score:

5 = Good

8 = Excellent

11 = Brilliant!

How many **ew** words can you find hidden in the box?

s	t	n	d	e	w	z	p
c	h	e	w	i	n	g	s
r	r	w	f	e	w	r	t
e	e	d	r	e	w	e	e
w	w	b	l	e	w	w	w

SPELLING *Extension*

When we put letters in **alphabetical order**, we first put them in the order of their first letters, like this: **dew   few   new**

If the first letters are the same, we then look at the second letters, like this:

a b ⓒd e f g ⓗi j k l m n o p q r s ⓣu v w x y z

s ⓒ rew   s ⓗ rew   s ⓣ ew

Write these words in alphabetical order.

Be careful with the last one!

1 few   flew

2 drew   dew

3 brew   blew   bow

4 grew   glue   give

5 crew   clue   cart   chair

6 new   knew   now

31

silent letters

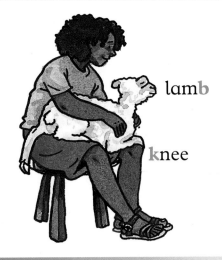

lamb

knee

key words

lamb
bomb
comb
climb
crumb
thumb

knee
kneel
knew
knife
knit
knot
knock

look say cover write check
check write cover say look

A Look at these picture clues.
Write the answer words in your book.

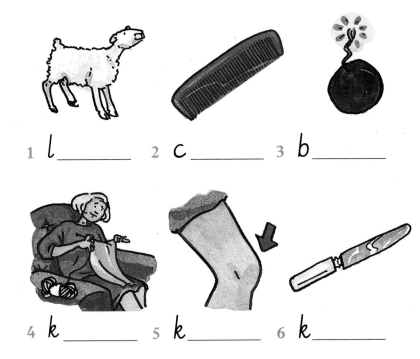

1 l_____   2 c_____   3 b_____

4 k_____   5 k_____   6 k_____

B Underline the letters you do not hear or say
when the words are read aloud.

C Write two other **silent letter** key words from
each family.

32

Adding endings to silent **b** words is easy, like this:

comb   comb**ing**   comb**ed**

Copy and finish this chart.

comb	combing	combed
bomb		
climb		
plumb		
lamb		

Be careful!
'Kneel' has **two**
vowels before the
last letter!

Adding endings to silent **k** words is sometimes not so simple. Sometimes we must double the last letter before we add **ing** or **ed** or **er**.

knit   knit**ting**   knit**ted**   knit**ter**

Look at the letter before the last letter.
Is it a single **vowel (a e i o u)**?

kn**i**t   yes   knitting   kno**c**k   no   knocking

A Copy and finish this chart.

knit	knitting		
knock		knocked	knocker
knot			
kneel			

B Write a sentence that has at least four 'silent k' words.

33

y
endings

baby  puppy

SPELLING *Focus*

key words

look say cover write check

check write cover say look

jelly
penny
berry
cherry
hobby
puppy

baby
lady
gravy
daisy
ivy
posy
story

A Look at these picture clues.
Write the answer words in your book.

1 j _____   2 p _____

3 b _____   4 l _____

B Write the key words that have double letters (like je**ll**y) neatly in your book.

C Write a sentence that uses at least two of the key words.

All the answers are key words.

A What am I?

1 I wag my tail when I'm pleased.
2 I grow on bushes.
3 I'm a small bunch of flowers.
4 I'm often found in a book.
5 I'm a very young child.
6 I wobble a lot!
7 I'm what you do in your spare time.
8 I'm good at climbing trees!

B Look at your reading book. Find six other nouns (name words) that end with **y**.

SPELLING *Extension*

Be careful! Number 6 is a tricky question.

All these words end in **y**.

| puppy story posy baby berry lady |

To make a word that ends in a consonant plus **y** plural, we change the **y** to **i** and add **es**, like this:

one pup**py**   three pup**pies**

Finish these captions. Write the plurals of the words in brackets.

1 two (pup_p_y)

2 three (sto_r_y)

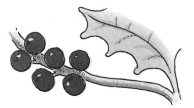

3 six (ber_r_y)

4 three (po_s_y)

5 two (ba_b_y)

6 four (da_y)

Check-up 2

A Write one word to describe what is happening in each of these pictures.
The first one is done to help you.

1 <u>barking</u>　　　2 s_____　　3 dr_____

4 y_____　　5 k_____　　6 c_____

B What are these?
They all end with **y**.

1 b_____　　2 j_____　　3 p_____

Remember, when we make **contractions** we make one word from two.

A Make contractions from these pairs of words.

1 should not   2 could not

3 you are

Use one of the contractions in a sentence.

B Add *d* or *ed* to each of these words.

1 store 2 form 3 force 4 scorch

C A silent letter is missing from each of these words. Write them correctly in your book.

1 bom_ 2 crum_ 3 _nit 4 _neel

SPELLING *Extension*

Remember, 'plural' means more than one.

A Write these words in alphabetical order.

1 wood good hood

2 patch match catch hatch

3 hound sound round ground

4 grew glue give

B

er fully ful ing ly ed d r

How many words can you make by adding the endings in the box to these words?
Write them in your book.

1 care   2 short   3 claw

4 climb 5 art

C Write the plurals of these words.

1 baby 2 puppy 3 berry 4 lady

ir
ire

bird

wire

SPELLING *Focus*

key words

look say cover write check

sir
stir
bird
third
dirt
shirt
skirt
first
thirst
fire
wire
tired

Look at these picture clues.
Write the **ir** words in your book.

1 st _____

2 b _____

3 sh _____

4 f _____

5 th _____

6 sk _____

38

Sort the key words into sound pattern families, like this, and write them in your book:

One of the families is much bigger than the other!

words with **ir** sounding like **fir**	words with **ire** sounding like **fire**
bird	fire

Write a sentence using one word from each family.

SPELLING *Extension*

Find each of these words in a dictionary.
Copy a **definition** of each one into your book.

A **definition** is a meaning of a word.

fire   hire   tired   wire

The first one is done for you.

fire – the heat from something burning

ur
ure

church

picture

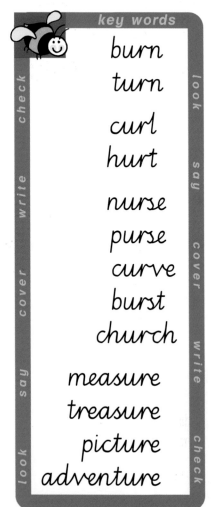

key words

burn
turn
curl
hurt
nurse
purse
curve
burst
church

measure
treasure
picture
adventure

look say cover write check *look say cover write check*

Find a **key word** to match each picture.
Write the words in your book.

1 c_____   2 h_____   3 n_____

4 p_____   5 b_____   6 p_____

Write a sentence about one of the pictures.

40

Copy these sentences.
Use key words to fill the gaps.

"Quick, Joe, _____ on the tap," shouted the chief.

"Help, the hose has _____!" shouted Joe.

"The flames are huge! Don't _____ yourself."

"Ouch, that _____!" yelled the firefighter.

"Get the _____ to put a dressing on your hand," called the chief.

v	s	e	m	b	u	r	n
f	u	r	e	y	p	x	g
t	r	e	a	s	u	r	e
u	f	t	s	u	r	h	h
r	n	n	u	r	s	e	u
n	r	s	r	e	e	l	r
o	x	p	e	c	u	r	l

Think whether you need to drop the final **e** before adding **ing**.

A Hidden in the puzzle box are 11 different **ur** words. Copy them into your book.

B Add *ing* to four of the words and write sentences using your new words.

41

ai
ay

The bat was forced to run aw**ay** –
The birds he could not face.
He now avoids the light of d**ay**
In shame and in disgrace.

Christopher Walker

SPELLING *Focus*

key words

look say cover write check

rail
sail
tail
nail
snail

aid
paid
maid

say
stay
tray
stray

look say cover write check

A Look at these picture clues.
Write the **ai** words in your book.

1 n_____   2 s_____   3 m_____

4 t_____   5 s_____   6 r_____

B Write four other **ai** key words neatly in
your book.

C Find two more **ai** words that are not in the list.

Remember, **compound** words are two smaller words joined, like this:

play + time = playtime

Use the words in the box to make compound words to match the clues.

> *stair rail rain hand play way*
> *ray run drop rail ground way*

1 falls from the sky *raindrop*

2 a place where we can play games

3 a set of wide steps

4 used by aeroplanes

5 helps when climbing the stairs

6 used by trains

Words that sound the same but have different spellings and meanings are called **homophones**.

Use your dictionary to decide which of each of these homophones matches the definition.

1 A woman servant *made* or *maid*

2 The movable end of an animal *tail* or *tale*

3 A bucket *pale* or *pail*

4 To speak to God *prey* or *pray*

Now write a definition for the homophones you **haven't** used.

ain
air

The **rain** in Sp**ain**
stays m**ain**ly in the pl**ain**.

SPELLING *Focus*

key words

look say cover write check

rain
train
strain
sprain

brain
drain
grain
stain
chain

air
pair
chair
stairs

look say cover write check

A Look at these picture clues.
Write the **ain** words in your book.

1 t _____

2 st _____

3 ch _____

4 dr _____

B Write six other **ain** key words neatly in
your book.

C Look at the rhyme.
Write the words that have the **ain** pattern.

pair	fair	hair	stairs
pear	fare	hare	stares

Copy these sentences. Use one of the homophones from the box to fill each gap. Check in your dictionary if you need help.

1 A ____ is a sweet, juicy fruit.

2 We pay a ____ to travel on a bus.

3 I like the swings best at the ____.

4 I have a new ____ of shoes.

5 My father ____ at me when he's cross.

6 We have lots of ____ to climb in our school.

7 I like my thick, black curly ____.

8 A ____ has powerful back legs and looks like a rabbit.

SPELLING *Extension*

craft	up	down	stairs	fair
port	way	mail	air	ground
hair	dresser	fun	arm	chair

The words in the box can be used to make ten compound words which have the **air** letter pattern. Write down as many as you can find, like this:

1 air + port = airport

igh

Dark n**igh**t
No l**igh**t
Not br**igh**t
Upt**igh**t
In fr**igh**t
Such pl**igh**t
I m**igh**t
Hide under the bedclothes.

Constance Milburn

SPELLING *Focus*

key words

look say cover write check

high
sigh

fight
might
night

light
flight

right
bright
fright

look say cover write check

A Look at these picture clues.
Write the **igh** words in your book.

 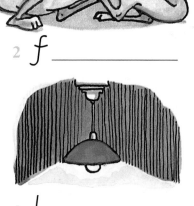

1 n_____ 2 f_____

3 t_____ 4 l_____

B Write five other **igh** key words neatly in
your book.

C Look at the poem.
Make a list of **igh** words that rhyme
with **night**.

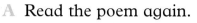

A Read the poem again.
Match a word from the poem to each clue.

Write the answers in your book. The first one is done to help you.

Use a dictionary to help you.

1 opposite of day = *night*
2 opposite of dim
3 maybe I will
4 reaches us from the sun
5 sudden fear

B Write three sentences using these words.

1 *sight*   2 *flight*   3 *right*

SPELLING *Extension*

> **Adjectives** are describing words.
> Sometimes we make special 'comparing' adjectives by adding **er** or **est**.

A Copy this box, and fill in the missing words. The first is done for you.

adjective

high	higher	highest
light		
tight		
bright		

B **igh** words have the same sound as many smaller words that end with **y**.
Write eight words that have similar spelling and which rhyme with **fly**.
Here are two to get you started: *cry sly*

Check-up 3

Look at these picture clues.
Write the words in your
book.

1 _____ 2 _____ 3 _____

A Make five compound words using the words in
the box.

rail hand way ground play fall rain drop

B What do these words mean? Write definitions in
your book.

1 *pear*   2 *pair*   3 *fair*   4 *fare*

A Add *ing* to each of these words.

1 *burn*   2 *nurse*   3 *turn*   4 *measure*

B Write these words in the order they would appear
in your dictionary.

1 *thirst   skirt   shirt*

2 *spray   sail   stray   snail*

3 *share   stairs   spare   saw*

C Divide these compound words to show the
smaller words from which they are made.

1 *armchair* 2 *fairground* 3 *airport*